D0493054

Amazing Planet Earth

MIGHTY RIVERS

JEN GREEN

W
FRANKLIN WATTS
LONDON · SYDNEY

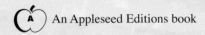 An Appleseed Editions book

First published in 2009 by Franklin Watts

Franklin Watts
338 Euston Road, London NW1 3BH

Franklin Watts Australia
Level 17/207 Kent St, Sydney, NSW 2000

© 2009 Appleseed Editions

Appleseed Editions Ltd
Well House, Friars Hill, Guestling, East Sussex TN35 4ET

Created by Q2AMedia
Editor: Katie Dicker
Art Director: Rahul Dhiman
Designer: Ranjan Singh
Picture Researcher: Shreya Sharma
Line Artist: Sibi N. Devasia
Colouring Artist: Mahender Kumar & Aadil Siddiqui

ISBN 978 0 7496 8806 6

Dewey classification: 551.48'3

All words in **bold** can be found in Glossary on pages 30–31.

Website information is correct at time of going to press. However, the publishers cannot
accept liability for any information or links found on third-party websites.

A CIP catalogue for this book is available from the British Library.

Picture credits
t=top b=bottom c=centre l=left r=right
Cover Images: Mirec/ Shutterstock.
Back Cove Image: Shutterstock

Insides: Kevin Tavares/ Shutterstock: Title Page, Dan Briski/ Shutterstock: 4, Mary Lane/ Shutterstock: 6, Robert Harding/ Robert
Harding World Imagery/ Corbis: 7, Jay Dickman/ Corbis: 8, Dave G. Houser/ Corbis: 9, Timothy Epp/ Shutterstock: 10, Neil Roy
Johnson/ Shutterstock: 11, Kevin Tavares/ shutterstock: 13, Laurin Rinder/ Shutterstock: 14, Kondrachov Vladimir/ Shutterstock: 15,
James M Phelps Jr/ Shutterstock: 16, Donald R. Swartz/ Shutterstock: 17, Carl & Ann Purcell/ Corbis: 18, Sue Darlow/ Fresh Food
Images/ Photolibrary: 19, Shutterstock: 21, Andrea Booher/ FEMA Photo: 22, Eric Draper/ Associated Press: 23, Steven Clevenger/
Corbis: 24, Dave Martin/ Associated Press: 25, Elisa Locci/ Shutterstock: 26, Maranso Gmbh/ iStockphoto: 27, Xinhua Press/ Corbis:
28. Elisa Locci/ Shutterstock: 31.
Q2A Media Art Bank: 5, 12, 20, 29.

Printed in China

Franklin Watts is a division of Hachette Children's Books,
an Hachette UK company.
www.hachette.co.uk

Contents

Raging rivers

Rivers are full of energy. They begin their life as small streams, but quickly grow into channels of fast-flowing water as they move and **meander** across the landscape.

Carving its journey

Mountain streams are fed by rainwater, melting ice or a **spring**. As they trickle over the land, the tiny streams join together to form a river. Soon, smaller rivers called **tributaries** add their fresh water, too. As the growing river follows its **course** downhill to a large lake or ocean, the water drags rocky fragments along, scouring the landscape as it flows.

- Some stretches of river water can flow at speeds of up to 15 km/h.

The water cycle

Rivers are essential to life on Earth as an important part of the water cycle. The sun's heat causes **water vapour** to rise from the oceans. As this moist air is blown across the land, it cools and condenses to form clouds. When it rains, water drains into rivers, which empty into the oceans, completing the cycle. This constant movement provides us with a steady supply of fresh water and helps to balance temperatures on Earth.

• Without rivers, the water cycle would break down.

DATA FILE

• Rivers flow on every continent except Antarctica, where all moisture is frozen.

• The world's shortest official river, the D River, Oregon, USA, is just 37 m long. That's about a third of the length of a football pitch!

• Some rivers, such as the Okavango River in Africa, never reach the ocean, but dry up in a swamp.

• Every day, the River Rhine in Europe carries over 4,000 cubic metres of mud to the North Sea.

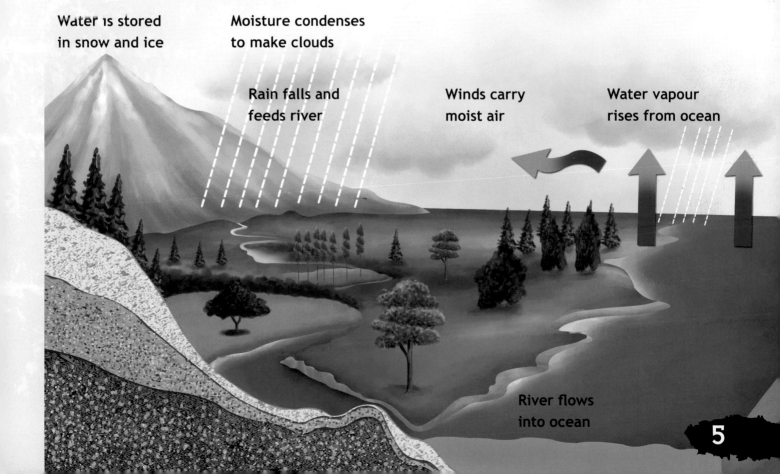

Water is stored in snow and ice

Moisture condenses to make clouds

Rain falls and feeds river

Winds carry moist air

Water vapour rises from ocean

River flows into ocean

The Nile

The Nile is the world's longest river. It flows from the mountains of East Africa to the Mediterranean Sea. The Nile is also a lifeline – without its waters, the surrounding land would turn to barren desert.

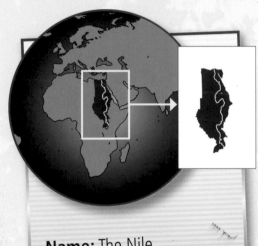

Name: The Nile
Location: North-east Africa
Length: 6,670 kilometres
River basin: Covers 3.3 million sq. km

An epic journey

The Nile's course is breathtaking. The river flows from Uganda to Egypt and together with its tributaries, flows through nine different countries. At its **mouth**, the river forms a **delta** that is 150 kilometres wide. In the vast dry deserts of Egypt, the Nile's floodwaters have produced fertile land. Civilisations have flocked to the river's banks since ancient times, and the Nile today provides a vital transport route.

- Settlements have grown up alongside the fertile banks of the Nile for centuries.

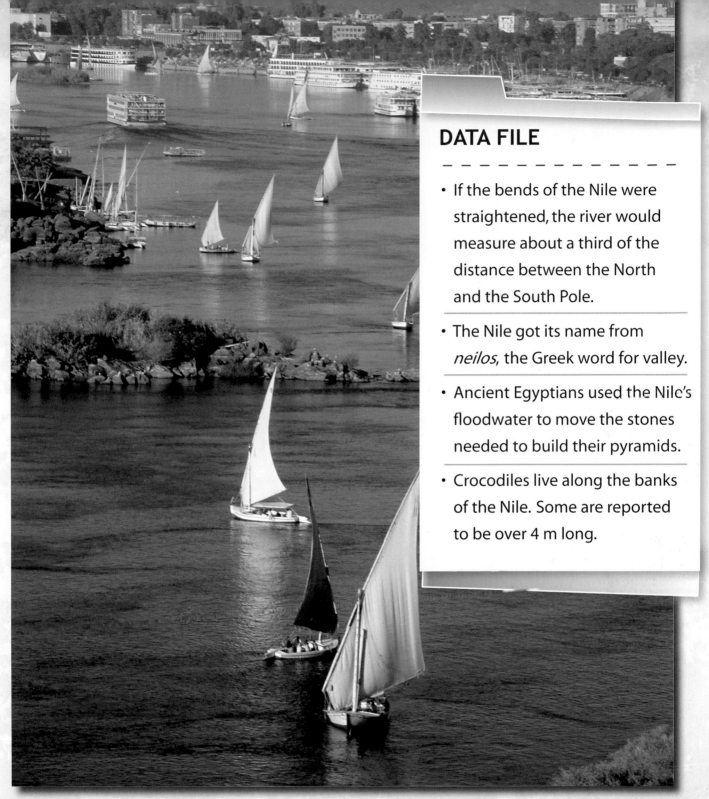

DATA FILE

- - - - - - - - - - - - -

- If the bends of the Nile were straightened, the river would measure about a third of the distance between the North and the South Pole.

- The Nile got its name from *neilos*, the Greek word for valley.

- Ancient Egyptians used the Nile's floodwater to move the stones needed to build their pyramids.

- Crocodiles live along the banks of the Nile. Some are reported to be over 4 m long.

Fertile floodwater

During the rainy season, many stretches of the Nile become a foaming torrent. When the river floods, it covers the surrounding land with fertile **silt**. The yearly flood allowed the civilisation of Ancient Egypt to grow up along the Nile. The area is ideal for farming, but if floodwaters get too high they can be very dangerous.

- People have fished and sailed on the Nile for thousands of years.

The Mighty Amazon

The Amazon is the world's second-longest river. Though slightly shorter than the Nile, it carries far more water. In fact, a fifth of all the world's river water flows along the Amazon.

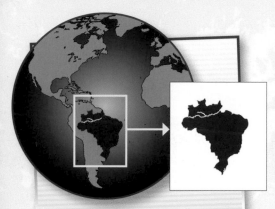

Name: The Amazon
Location: South America
Length: 6,448 kilometres
River basin: Covers 7,180,000 sq. km

Rainforest adventure

On the Amazon's long journey from its **source** high in the Andes mountains to the Atlantic Ocean, the river is joined by over 1,000 tributaries. Often, these are large rivers themselves. They combine to form a mighty river that flows east through the largest rainforest in the world. The Amazon is home to a wide range of wildlife, from flesh-eating fish called piranhas, to river dolphins and huge snakes called anacondas. Although the rainforest has restricted the development of cities along the river's banks, the Amazon has been a trade route for centuries.

• For most of its length, the Amazon flows through a vast tropical rainforest.

Wide waters

The Amazon has the world's largest **drainage basin**, covering 7,180,000 sq. km. That's nearly half of South America! In its lower course, it becomes impossible to see from one bank of the river to the other. During the rainy season, the river reaches depths of up to 40 metres and can be up to 45 kilometres wide. The river is so wide and deep that ocean-going ships can sail upriver as far as the port of Manaus, 1,000 kilometres from the Atlantic Ocean. When the river finally reaches the sea it is about 240 kilometres wide.

News Flash

September 2006

A new study suggests that the Amazon once flowed in the opposite direction to its present course! Rock samples from the riverbed show that during the age of the dinosaurs, 145 to 65 million years ago, the river rose in a range of mountains in the east, and flowed west toward the Pacific, carrying **sediment** to the centre of South America.

• The Amazon is so wide that huge ships can travel along much of its course.

In the hills

In their upper course, young rivers hurtle down over steep, rocky slopes. The rushing water wears away the land to form dramatic features such as canyons, rapids and waterfalls. This natural wearing process is called **erosion**.

A river's load

As streams and rivers gush downhill, they loosen rocks and soil along their banks, which are swept away. Stones and rocks bouncing along the riverbed increase the rate of erosion. These rocky fragments are called the river's **load**.

The speed of erosion depends on the hardness of the riverbed. Soft rocks get worn away more quickly than hard rocks. The steepness of the ground also affects how fast the river flows.

- The Yellowstone River in Wyoming, USA, has carved a deep, V-shaped valley.

Powerful action

As the river flows down the hills, it cuts deeper and deeper. In time, the foaming water wears a deep, V-shaped valley. Rapids form where the river churns over large boulders in shallow water. Meanwhile, the rocks swept along by the current are gradually smashed into very fine pieces, called sediment. The sediment floats in the water, while the large boulders are dragged along the riverbed.

• Gushing water carries a river's load – from huge boulders to fine sediment.

DATA FILE

• The Kali Gandaki Gorge in Nepal is one of the world's deepest **gorges** at 5.5 km deep. It has been carved by a river flowing between two of the world's ten highest mountains.

• The world's highest waterfall is Angel Falls in Venezuela, South America. The River Churun plunges 979 m over a rocky shelf.

• The widest waterfalls lie on the River Khone in Laos, in south-east Asia. The falls are over 10 km wide.

Niagara Falls

Niagara Falls between Canada and the United States is one of the world's most famous waterfalls. The Niagara River plunges 53 metres into a cauldron of foaming water. Misty spray shoots high in the air.

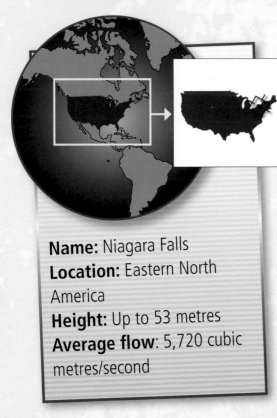

Name: Niagara Falls
Location: Eastern North America
Height: Up to 53 metres
Average flow: 5,720 cubic metres/second

Eroding rocks

Waterfalls form where a river flows over a band of hard rock such as granite, on to softer rock such as shale. The soft rocks wear away more quickly, creating a sheer cliff. At Niagara Falls, the falling water has also worn a deep **plunge pool** at the base. The current flows fastest near the centre of the channel, wearing the rocks there more quickly. This has created the curving horseshoe-shape of the falls. Niagara Falls is extremely wide. Around 5,720 cubic metres of water plunges to its base every second.

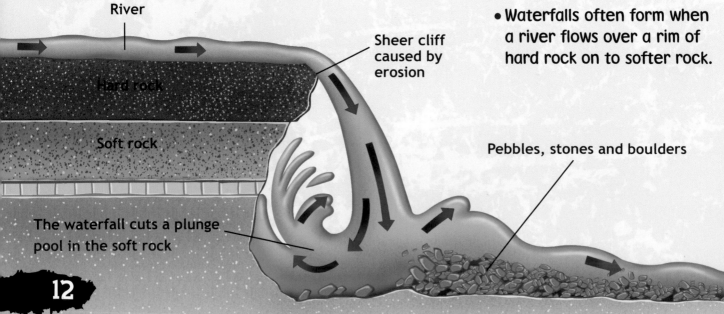

River

Sheer cliff caused by erosion

Hard rock

Soft rock

The waterfall cuts a plunge pool in the soft rock

Pebbles, stones and boulders

- Waterfalls often form when a river flows over a rim of hard rock on to softer rock.

Moving upstream

Niagara Falls began to form at the end of the last **Ice Age**, when the ice sheets covering North America melted. A raging torrent of meltwater gushed down from Lake Erie, carving the waterfall. As the erosion continued, fast-flowing water ate into soft rocks at the base of the falls to create an overhang. Later this ledge of rock collapsed, and the waterfall moved a little upstream. This process has happened many times. The falls are now shifting towards Lake Erie at the rate of about a metre a year.

News Flash

29 March 1848

This week for an amazing 30 hours, the roar of Niagara Falls was silenced. Huge slabs of ice at Lake Erie created a jam which blocked the river. The falls ran dry, and a few brave souls explored the riverbed on foot or horseback. Then, with a mighty roar, the river broke free again and thundered over the falls. Niagara was back in business.

- Some say the name Niagara comes from a Native American word meaning 'thundering waters'.

The Grand Canyon

The Grand Canyon in North America is one of the world's most spectacular canyons. Its steep sides were carved, in part, by the action of the mighty Colorado River over millions of years.

Name: The Grand Canyon
Location: Western North America
Height: Up to 1.6 kilometres deep
Length: 350 kilometres long
Width: 30 kilometres wide

A staircase through time

The Grand Canyon is a vast expanse that reveals the spectacular power of nature. The canyon is not completely sheer, but descends in small steps, like a staircase. The steps are made of layers of hard and soft rocks, which have worn away at different rates over time.

● **The Grand Canyon reveals billions of years of the Earth's history in its worn rock faces.**

Layers of rock

The Grand Canyon was formed by two main forces: erosion and **uplift** – the tremendous force that builds mountains. Millions of years ago, the Colorado River flowed over layers of rock that were being uplifted. As a rocky plateau rose upwards, the river cut even deeper, forming an awesome canyon. Bands of grey limestone, yellow sandstone, pink granite and grey shale give the canyon its rainbow colours. The rocks at the top are the youngest – around 250 million years old, which is young by the Earth's standards. The rocks at the bottom are incredibly ancient – about 2 billion years old. Gazing down into the canyon is like looking back through time to Earth's distant past.

News Flash

20 March 2007

This week saw the opening of the Skywalk, a glass-bottomed walkway that extends 20 m beyond the rim of the Grand Canyon. The curving walkway allows sightseers to gaze down to the valley floor 1,220 m below. The glass floor is so clear one visitor said: "it was like walking on a cloud".

• The Colorado River's strong current erodes the riverbed and carries everything in its path downstream.

In the valley

In their middle course, rivers leave the hills and begin to flow through gently rolling country. Streams make the river bigger and wider and the water starts to weave from side to side.

Bends and loops

As the river glides along smoothly, it begins to drop its load. This is called **deposition**. Large, heavy rocks are dropped first, then smaller stones and gravel. As the river curls around bends, the water flows fastest on the outside, eating into the bank. Sand and gravel are dropped on the inside, where the current is slowest. Over time, shallow curves become great loops called meanders. Eventually, the current breaks through the narrow neck of the loop and continues its course, leaving an **oxbow lake**.

• Horseshoe Bend in Arizona, USA, is a deep bend worn by the Colorado River.

Ocean features

In its lower course, the river wanders through a wide, flat valley called a flood plain. Fine sediment dumped by floodwaters makes this area very fertile. As the river approaches the sea, it flows through a wide **estuary**. **Mudflats** are created on each side as the river deposits its silt. When it reaches the sea, the river dumps the remaining sediment to form features such as islands, **spits** and deltas. The river's movement means the land is constantly changing.

DATA FILE

- The Huang He (Yellow River) in China is the world's muddiest river. The water is coloured by vast quantities of yellow soil that have washed in from its banks.

- The largest oxbow lake in North America is Lake Chicot. This crescent-shaped lake was once a loop of the Mississippi River.

- In Australia, oxbow lakes are known as billabongs.

- Many cities have grown up by rivers as they approach the sea. New York City, USA, is on the banks of the Hudson River which flows into the Atlantic Ocean.

The Ganges Delta

The world's largest delta has formed at the mouths of the Ganges and Brahmaputra rivers in India and Bangladesh, in southern Asia. This vast, swampy expanse covers an area bigger than Holland and Belgium combined.

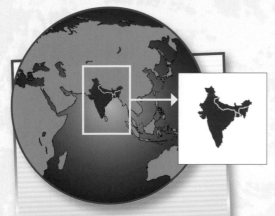

Name: Ganges and Brahmaputra Delta
Location: India and Bangladesh
Area: Covers 75,000 sq. km

Channels to the sea

The Ganges Delta is 350 kilometres wide when the river water drains into the Bay of Bengal. This low-lying swampy area is made of silt dumped by the Ganges and Brahmaputra rivers. This silt is left when the rivers slow down and meet near the ocean. The rivers split into smaller channels as they wind through the sandy deposits, causing the delta to look like an enormous fan.

• The Ganges Delta is full of water channels that wind their way towards the ocean.

Friend or foe?

The rich silt of the Ganges Delta makes it extremely fertile. The delta is the most populated river basin in the world. Over 140 million people live in this area, with its fertile farmland and constant supply of fresh water. Cheap river transport has meant that many cities have also grown up in the region. Fishing is popular, and crops such as rice, tea and jute are grown. Farmers are able to get up to three harvests a year from the rich soil. However, this low-lying region is at great risk of flooding after heavy rain. Rising sea levels in the future are also set to make the area even more dangerous.

News Flash

16 July 2004

This summer has seen the worst floods in India and Bangladesh for many decades. Very heavy seasonal rains have caused the flooding, which covers two-thirds of Bangladesh. Over a thousand people have died, and an incredible 8.5 million homes have been damaged. The governments of the stricken nations are supplying food aid by helicopter.

• Rice is grown in flooded fields, called paddies, on the Ganges Delta.

Dangerous rivers

Villages, towns and cities have grown up beside rivers that offer fertile land and convenient transport. However, these areas are also very dangerous. Over the centuries, floods have killed millions of people.

Weather warnings

Floods often strike after heavy rain swells a river, causing water levels to rise. Eventually, the river bursts its banks and spreads over the surrounding land. In cold, snowy parts of the world, warm spring weather brings a thaw, and melted snow fills the river. In tropical regions, seasonal winds called **monsoons** bring torrential rain. High in the mountains, a violent thunderstorm can transform a small stream into a raging torrent in just minutes. This produces a sudden and dangerous **flash flood**.

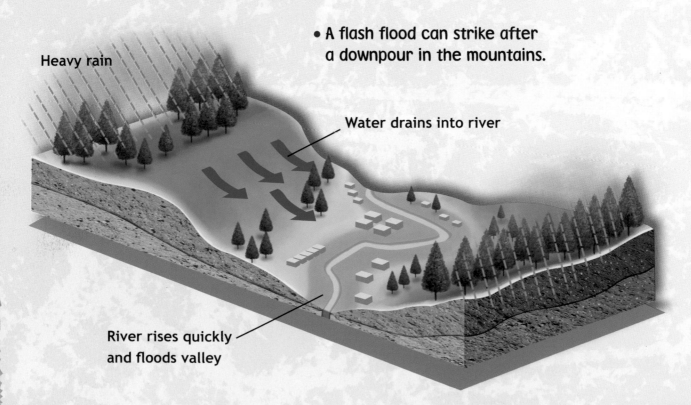

• A flash flood can strike after a downpour in the mountains.

Heavy rain

Water drains into river

River rises quickly and floods valley

Defence measures

Rivers bring fertility to a region but if the river floods, the raging water can be very destructive. Muddy water can swirl into buildings, leaving a tide of black mud and causing severe damage. Floodwaters also carry the risk of disease, especially if the water is tainted with **sewage**. Along many rivers, high banks called **levees** are built to try to prevent flooding. Other rivers are dammed or **dredged** to make them deeper, but these defences do not always work.

- Floodwater can wreck vehicles and buildings, and endanger lives.

News Flash

August 1996

A flash flood high in the Pyrenees mountains in northern Spain has killed 87 people, and 180 more are injured. The disaster struck after a severe thunderstorm caused a cloudburst, and 8 cm of rain fell in just two hours. A wall of water swept down a mountain stream and into a campsite. Bodies were recovered from 16 km downstream.

Mississippi floods

The Mississippi is North America's greatest river. It carries millions of tonnes of **freight** a year, and is vital to the region's prosperity. Farms, towns and factories line the river. However in 1993, flooding along the Mississippi brought great destruction.

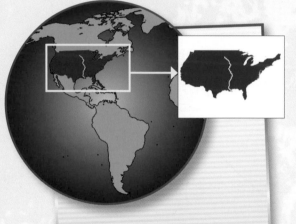

Name: The Mississippi
Location: North America
Length: 3,666 kilometres
River basin: Covers
3.1 million sq. km

Record rainfall

In the spring of 1993, the area around the Mississippi river basin experienced frequent storms and record rainfall. Combined with the heavy snowfall of the previous winter, the river began to swell uncontrollably. In its lower course, the Mississippi creates natural levees of mud and gravel along its banks. But these levees, and additional flood defences, could not protect the riverbank towns from flooding.

• In 1993, the Mississippi rose nearly 6 metres higher than usual causing devastating floods.

Rising waters

The floodwaters covered 80,000 sq. km of land. People stacked millions of sandbags to try to contain the water, but in vain. Some 75 towns were flooded, city streets became channels of rushing water and fields resembled lakes. It was like a scene from a disaster movie. When people returned to their homes, they began the painful task of clearing the debris. But for some there was no going back – around 10,000 homes had been destroyed.

• A man bails water from behind a barrier formed by sandbags during the Mississippi flood.

News Flash

December 1994

A man was imprisoned for life today for contributing to some of the worst flooding in the Mississippi region. James Scott removed sandbags from a levee during the disaster because he wanted to strand his wife on the other side while he went to a party. His actions caused the Mississippi to flood 56 sq. km of farmland and destroyed hundreds of buildings.

Hurricane Katrina

In 2005, disaster returned to the Mississippi, this time in the wake of a powerful **hurricane**. On 29 August, Hurricane Katrina blew in from the Gulf of Mexico. The immensely powerful winds devastated coastal towns in their path. The calm 'eye' of the hurricane, in the centre of the swirling winds, also formed an area of low pressure that sucked up a mound of water below it. This created a very high tide called a storm surge. The storm surge and torrential rain caused the Mississippi to break its banks. The floodwaters overpowered the levees protecting the port of New Orleans and gushed into the city. Nearly 2,000 people died in the hurricane and the floods that followed.

- Around 80 per cent of the city of New Orleans was flooded in the aftermath of Hurricane Katrina.

Rescue work

The authorities were slow to react to the disaster, and it was days before people were rescued and taken to emergency shelters. Most of the major roads in and out of the city were badly damaged, which meant that the only way to reach the stricken area was by boat or plane. The army began to repair the levees and pump water out of the city, but it took months before people could return and rebuild their lives. New Orleans is built on low-lying, marshy ground and is almost completely surrounded by water. The city's flood defences have now been strengthened, but if another hurricane scored a direct hit, flooding would be likely again.

News Flash

31 August 2005

The city of New Orleans has been hit by one of the worst floods on record. The authorities ordered people to leave before the hurricane struck – but with no buses or trains running, many people were stranded. More than a thousand are believed dead. Survivors have climbed on to the roofs of houses, from where they are being rescued by helicopter and boat.

• Frightened survivors are rescued by boat and helped to safety.

Changing rivers

Rivers are constantly changing. Heavy rain and melted snow can swell a river, while a **drought** can make it dry up completely. Floods and erosion cause rivers to change direction but people can change the flow of rivers, too.

Changing weather

In many parts of the world, rivers are affected by seasonal changes. Some rivers freeze over in winter, while many flood in spring. Long, hot summers can cause rivers to dwindle to a trickle. In the future, temperature changes caused by **global warming** are likely to make conditions even more extreme. Some regions are getting wetter, making floods more likely. Others are at risk of drought.

• This stranded boat in Sweden has been trapped by frozen river water. In future, global warming may make extreme weather more likely around the world.

Human-made changes

People can alter rivers, too. We build high banks to prevent flooding, or dredge the riverbed to make it deeper. We dig **canals** to join two rivers, or to link a river to the sea. People also build power stations to capture the energy of river water. The river is dammed to direct the flow of water past giant wheels called **turbines**. These spin to work generators that produce electricity. We call this **hydroelectricity**.

● The Glen Canyon Dam towers over the Colorado River in Arizona, USA. A huge reservoir stores water for this dry region and the dam generates electricity.

DATA FILE

- In China, people began digging a long canal to link the Yellow and Yangtze rivers in around 500 BC. By the 1300s, the Grand Canal network was 1,780 km long.

- In 1959, the St Lawrence Seaway was opened in North America. This network of canals was built to allow ships to pass from the Great Lakes to the Atlantic Ocean.

- According to a United Nations' report, the Himalayan glaciers that feed into the Ganges River, could vanish by 2030 because of global warming.

- Huge areas of land are flooded to make a dam's **reservoir**. When plants begin to rot in the floodwater they release methane, a gas that contributes to global warming.

The Three Gorges Dam

The world's largest dam has recently been built on a dramatic section of the Yangtze River in China. The Three Gorges Dam will help to prevent flooding and will generate electricity for the city of Shanghai.

Name: The Yangtze
Location: China
Length: 6,379 kilometres
River basin: Covers 1.8 million sq. km

A huge project

The Yangtze is the world's third-largest river. The dam has been built downstream from the Three Gorges – a series of narrow canyons where the water can run very deep. This huge engineering project took over ten years to build and cost almost US$30 billion. But when the power station is working fully in 2011, it will supply a tenth of China's electricity.

• The Three Gorges Dam is a vast structure, over 180 metres high and 2 kilometres wide.

Changing the landscape

The Three Gorges Dam brings many benefits, but the project has brought great changes to the landscape. A massive reservoir, 650 kilometres long, was built behind the dam. As the water level rose, the lake flooded several historic cities, and over a million people had to abandon their homes and move elsewhere. The reservoir will supply water to farms, cities and industries. A huge network of canals is being built to transfer water from the Yangtze River to cities in the north of China.

News Flash

23 July 2008

Nearly 1,000 households have been moved in Gaoyang town to make way for the rising waters of the Three Gorges Dam reservoir. More than 1.4 million people have now been relocated. The dam is designed to prevent flooding and to generate electricity. However, there are concerns that the reservoir is polluted and that landslides are becoming more common.

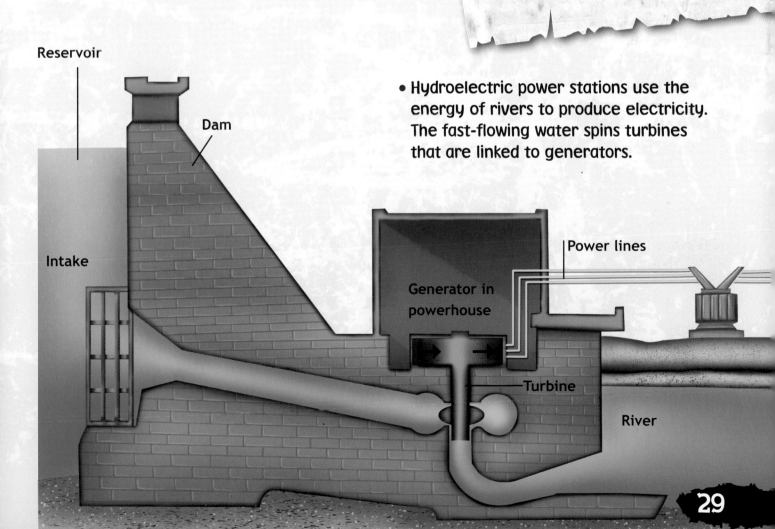

Reservoir

Dam

Intake

- Hydroelectric power stations use the energy of rivers to produce electricity. The fast-flowing water spins turbines that are linked to generators.

Power lines

Generator in powerhouse

Turbine

River

Glossary

canal an artificial waterway

course a river's journey. Also called the upper, middle and lower course

delta a flat, swampy area on the coast made of sediment dropped by a river

deposition when a river drops its load of rock and sediment

drainage basin the total area drained by a river and its tributaries

dredge to deepen or widen a river by digging. This can reduce the risk of flooding or make it easier for ships to pass

drought a long time without rain

erosion when rock or soil is worn away by natural forces

estuary the mouth or lower part of a river, which is entered by seawater at high tide

flash flood a sudden flood that happens after very heavy rain, often in the mountains or a desert

freight goods transported by water, rail, road or air

global warming a general rise in world temperatures, caused by a build-up of pollution in the atmosphere

gorge a deep, narrow valley with sheer, vertical sides

hurricane a huge, very powerful storm with whirling winds

hydroelectricity electricity that is made using energy from fast-flowing water

Ice Age a period in the Earth's history when the climate was cooler than today. The last Ice Age ended about 10,000 years ago

levee a high bank edging a river, made of sediment dropped by the river when it floods

load the rocky fragments carried along by a river, including mud, sand, stones and boulders

meander a wide, curving bend on a river

monsoon a tropical wind that changes direction, bringing rain at a certain time of year

mouth where a river empties into the sea or a lake

mudflat a low-lying bank along the lower course of a river, made of mud or silt

oxbow lake a crescent-shaped lake that forms when a meander is cut off from a river

plunge pool the deep pool found at the base of a waterfall, carved by falling water and churning rocks

reservoir an artificial lake created by a dam, and used to store water

sediment fine rocky material, such as sand or mud

sewage dirty water from homes, containing human waste

silt fine pieces of rock that have been ground down to torm sand or mud

source the place where a river begins, such as a spring or lake

spit a slender finger of land stretching out into the sea or a river, and made of sediment

spring a small stream of water flowing naturally from the Earth

tributary a minor river or stream that joins the main river

turbine a machine powered by steam, gas or water, used to generate electricity

uplift when the rocks of the Earth's crust are raised upward by upheaval deep inside the Earth

water vapour water in the form of a gas

Index

Webfinder

www.bbc.co.uk/schools/riversandcoasts/index.shtml
An introduction to rivers and the water cycle

http://ga.water.usgs.gov/edu/
Facts about water on Earth – where water is found and how it is used

http://internationalrivers.org/
Learn about rivers and dams around the world

www.ukrivers.net/education.html
Facts about rivers and related environmental issues

www.nationalgeographic.com/geography-action/ga01.html
A look at river systems and their impact on the environment